MAY YOU ENJOY THIS BOOK

The Public Library is free to all cardholders.
You can increase its usefulness to all by returning
books promptly, on or before the "Date Due".

If you derive pleasure and profit from the use of
your public library, please tell others about its
many services.

TECHNOWORLD

Satellites and Communications

Ian Graham

RAINTREE
STECK-VAUGHN
RSVP PUBLISHERS

A Harcourt Company

Austin   New York
www.raintreesteckvaughn.com

Published by Raintree Steck-Vaughn Publishers, an imprint of Steck-Vaughn Company

Library of Congress Cataloging-in-Publication Data

Graham Ian, 1953-
Satellites and communications / Ian Graham.
    p. cm.-- (Technoworld)
    Includes bibliographical references and index.
    ISBN 0-7398-3255-7
    1. Artificial satellites in telecommunication--Juvenile literature.
    [1.Artificial satellites in telecommunication.] I. Title. II. Series

    TK5104 G73 2001
    621.382'5--dc21   00-055242

Printed in Italy. Bound in the United States.
1 2 3 4 5 6 7 8 9 0 LB 05 04 03 02 01

CONTENTS

TELECOMMUNICATIONS

Telecommunication means sending information a long distance with the help of equipment such as telephones and human-made satellites. A satellite is an unmanned spacecraft in orbit around the Earth.

Thanks to high-speed telecommunications, we can watch important events, such as sports competitions, live on television. Reports of events in remote places used to take days to reach us. Nowadays, television shows us what is happening all over the world almost instantly.

WAVES, WIRES, AND FIBERS

Telecommunications travel around the world in different ways. Radio is used to communicate with satellites, because only radio waves can travel through empty space.

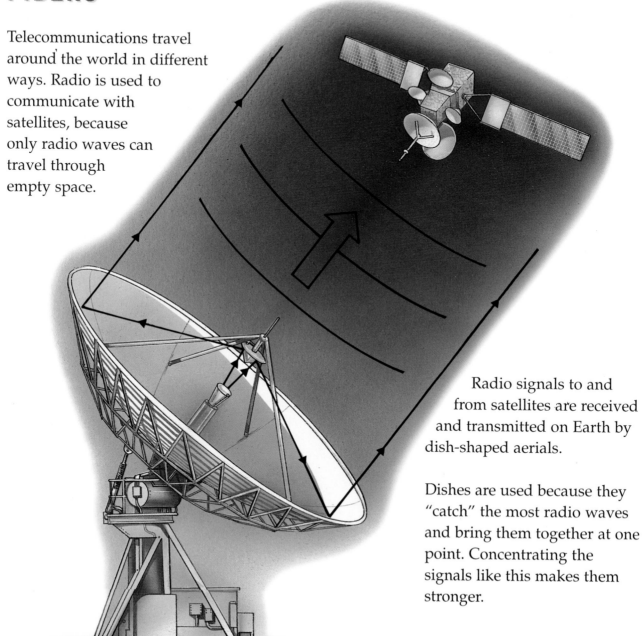

Radio signals to and from satellites are received and transmitted on Earth by dish-shaped aerials.

Dishes are used because they "catch" the most radio waves and bring them together at one point. Concentrating the signals like this makes them stronger.

Telephone Calls

Telephone calls travel along metal cables as electric currents. Fiber-optic cables carry them as light beams along glass fibers. Radio waves carry them between aerials on the ground and satellites in space.

▶ **Radio antennas are attached to tall towers so that they are higher than surrounding buildings and trees. One tower may have lots of antennas pointing in different directions.**

How Do Optical Fibers Work?

Optical fibers are thin strands of glass. Light beams carrying telephone calls travel down the center of a fiber without leaking out through the sides. A light detector picks them up at the other end.

Optical cables are made from thin glass fibers that can bend without breaking. Light travels down each fiber and comes out at the other end.

Modern telecommunications began with the electric telegraph during the nineteenth century. It worked by sending electric currents along wires. In 1876, Alexander Graham Bell invented a new type of telegraph, the telephone. Radio was developed by Guglielmo Marconi in the 1890s. By the early 1900s, telegraph messages and telephone calls were being sent by radio, too. Then in 1925, John Logie Baird succeeded in sending pictures by radio and invented television.

TECHNOFACT

The First Phone Call

On March 10, 1876, Alexander Graham Bell made the world's first telephone call to his assistant in another room, Thomas Watson. He said to him, "Mr. Watson, come here, I want to see you."

Communications Satellites

The first communications satellite was *Echo 1*, launched in 1960. It was a metal-coated balloon that reflected radio waves. In 1962 *Telstar* transmitted the first live television pictures across the Atlantic Ocean.

Name: *Telstar*
Launched: 1962

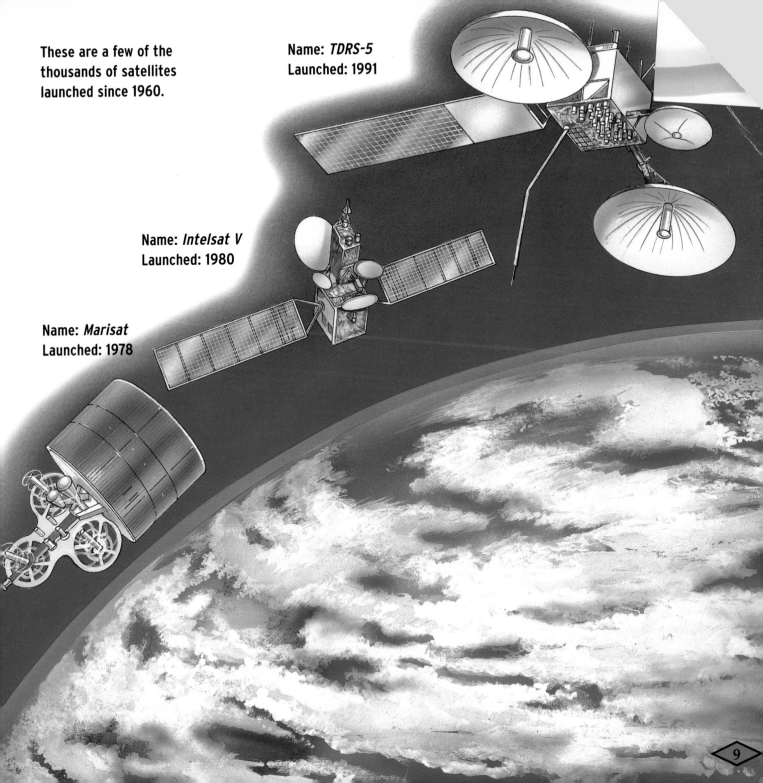

These are a few of the thousands of satellites launched since 1960.

Name: *TDRS-5*
Launched: 1991

Name: *Intelsat V*
Launched: 1980

Name: *Marisat*
Launched: 1978

HOW COMMUNICATIONS WORK

Communications satellites are box- or cylinder-shaped. Cylindrical satellites are covered with solar cells, while box-shaped satellites have winglike solar panels. Communications satellites use a special orbit, called a geostationary orbit, 22,370 mi (36,000 km) above the equator. The satellite orbits as fast as the Earth spins, so it stays over the same spot on Earth.

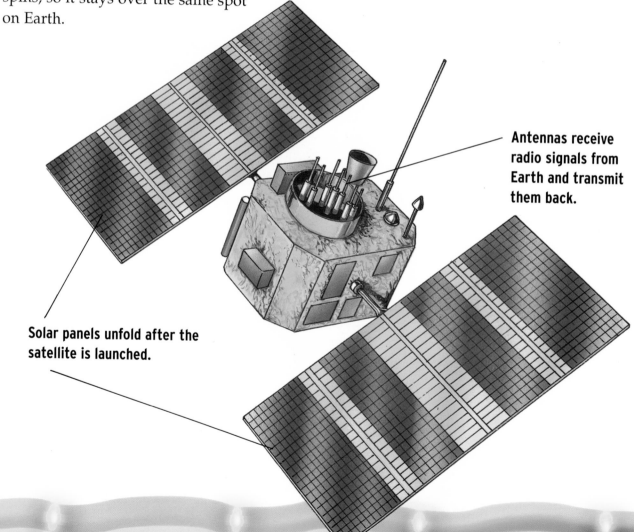

Antennas receive radio signals from Earth and transmit them back.

Solar panels unfold after the satellite is launched.

The Parts of a
Communications Satellite

All the parts of a satellite are built on a strong main frame. One part, the power system, produces the electricity it needs from sunlight using solar cells. Another part, the payload, is the equipment carried by the satellite—its radio transmitters and receivers. The attitude control system keeps the satellite in the correct position, with its aerials pointing toward Earth.

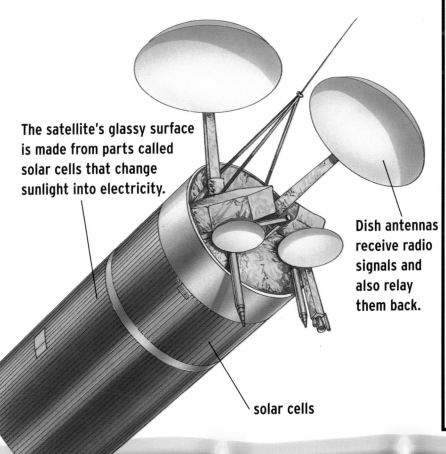

The satellite's glassy surface is made from parts called solar cells that change sunlight into electricity.

Dish antennas receive radio signals and also relay them back.

solar cells

HOW DOES MY TELEPHONE WORK?

The number you tap into your telephone tells the telephone network which country, city, area, and telephone number you want to be connected to.

Analog and Digital

Your telephone makes an electrical copy of your voice. This is an analog signal. For most of its journey, your voice travels in a different way—as a digital signal, a code of numbers.

A special type of telephone line, an ISDN (Integrated Services Digital Network) line, is digital all the way from one end to the other.

A microphone in the mouthpiece changes your voice into electricity. The earpiece changes electric currents received by the telephone into sound.

Mobile and Cordless

Mobile telephones communicate by radio with a nearby aerial. The aerials are linked by radio waves to computers, which connect the calls to their destinations. A cordless phone handset communicates by radio with its own base unit just a few feet away.

Mobile phones have a small screen that shows information like the date, the time, and details of the call being made or received.

Textphones

Textphones or minicoms are special telephones used by deaf people. A person communicates with a caller by typing words into the telephone, which appear on a screen at the same time.

ON THE BOX

Television programs are carried to our homes in two ways—by radio waves and by fiber-optic cables. The radio waves come from aerials on the ground or satellites in space. The television set changes the signals it receives into lines of colored dots that join together to make a picture.

High Definition Television

One way of making television pictures better is to pack more lines of colored dots into them. This is called high definition television, or HDTV.

Better screen quality means that watching TV is now as exciting as going to the movies.

Digital Television

Digital television transmits programs in digital code. This is simply a stream of numbers that the television set has to decode. It offers clearer pictures and dozens more channels.

Satellite TV systems use a dish to "catch" radio waves from a satellite and a decoder to change them into a form that a TV set understands.

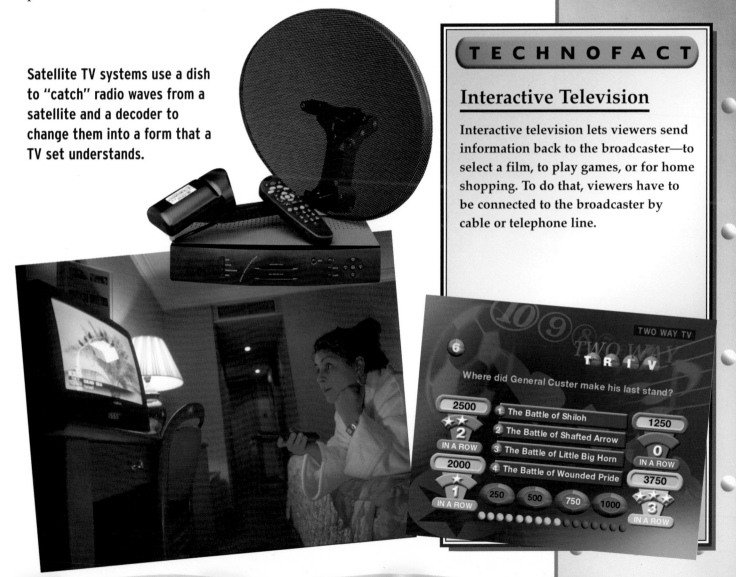

TWO WAY TV

TWO WAY TRIV

6

Where did General Custer make his last stand?

2500

2 IN A ROW

1 The Battle of Shiloh

2 The Battle of Shafted Arrow

3 The Battle of Little Big Horn

4 The Battle of Wounded Pride

1250

0 IN A ROW

2000

1 IN A ROW

250 500 750 1000

3750

3 IN A ROW

ON-LINE COMMUNICATION

On-line communication means contacting people by linking your computer with theirs through normal telephone lines. When many computers are linked in this way, a network is formed. The world's biggest and best-known computer network is the Internet. Anyone with a computer and a modem can use it. The Internet links up computers all over the world using telephone lines and satellites to send information.

Schoolchildren can visit a zoo without leaving their desks.

E-mail and the Web

If you have a computer and a modem, you can send someone an electronic letter, or e-mail. The World Wide Web is a collection of Internet sites, or Web pages, where you can find out information about almost any subject just by searching the Internet, or "browsing."

VIDEO LINKS

Hearing someone's voice over the phone is not as exciting as seeing them at the same time. Videophones are telephones fitted with a video camera and a screen so that callers can see each other as they talk. A computer fitted with a video camera and connected to the Internet can also be used as a videophone.

Videophones are fitted with a tiny video camera and screen.

Videoconferencing

To save people from traveling long distances for meetings, they can be linked together electronically in a videoconference, or teleconference. Each person in the meeting appears as a video picture with sound in the other person's room.

Businesspeople can avoid many hours of traveling by meeting with foreign colleagues at a videoconference.

Internet Video

Short video clips and animations can be sent through the Internet. Video cameras linked to the Web can show live pictures on the Internet from all over the world. Videophone calls can also be made using the Internet. But until we have faster Internet connections, the pictures will be small and jerky.

A camera linked to the Internet shows live pictures of a New York City street.

COMMUNICATIONS IN ACTION

People on the move can find out where they are by communicating with satellites. Drivers can avoid traffic jams by using a system that guides them around trouble spots.

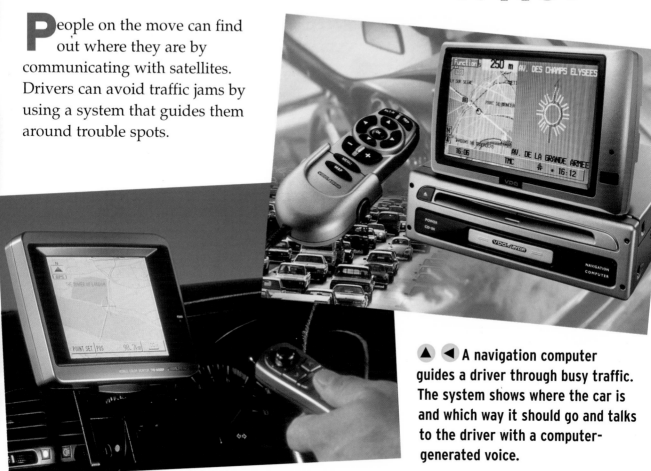

▲ ◀ A navigation computer guides a driver through busy traffic. The system shows where the car is and which way it should go and talks to the driver with a computer-generated voice.

Air-traffic Control

Airplanes are guided through the sky by air-traffic controllers, who track the planes by radar. Radar works by sending out radio waves, which are reflected by the aircraft. The reflections appear on a radar screen.

Satellite Navigation

The Global Positioning System (GPS) tells travelers where they are anywhere in the world. A GPS receiver picks up radio signals from navigation satellites. It uses them to calculate a person's exact position.

T E C H N O F A C T

In-flight Communication

Airline passengers can make telephone calls and send faxes. The radio signals are received by communications satellites, which relay them to ground stations linked to the telephone network.

EMERGENCY COMMUNICATIONS

Emergency services rely heavily on two-way radio communication. Rescues can be complicated operations involving several police, rescue, and medical services working together. They all keep in touch with each other by radio.

▶ **A doctor keeps in touch with a hospital by radio during an emergency flight.**

CCTV

Closed Circuit Television (CCTV) uses electronic cameras to send pictures to one or a few TV screens, instead of broadcasting them to everyone. CCTV cameras are often used to detect crimes in stores and streets.

SOS

For most of the 20th century, ships in distress either transmitted Morse code for the letters SOS or gave the voice message "Mayday." Now, ships in distress transmit their position automatically. All a crew member has to do is press a button that triggers a radio message containing the ship's name and position.

A security camera detects a crime. A controller watching the pictures guides police to the location.

ON THE MOVE

We used to depend on fixed telephones and desktop computers for communication. Now, mobile phones and portable computers are small enough to be taken anywhere. No one need be out of touch anymore, wherever they are.

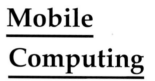

Mobile Computing

With a portable computer and a mobile phone, you can connect to the Internet wherever you are. The beach or the park can be your office.

Thanks to miniature battery-powered radio and electric circuits, computers and telephones can now be made small enough to fit in a pocket.

Satellite Phones

Today, mobile phones have to be within range of an aerial to work. However, a new type of mobile phone works anywhere on Earth, because the radio aerials that relay its signals are in space, onboard satellites.

Future mobile phones will be linked by radio to a swarm of satellites in orbit around the Earth.

People who move around in their work often carry pagers so they can be contacted wherever they are.

Pagers

Pagers receive messages by radio. The messages appear as text on a tiny screen. The pager beeps when it receives a message. Doctors and vets often carry pagers to call them to emergencies. If people do not want to be disturbed by ringing noises, they can set their pagers to vibrate instead.

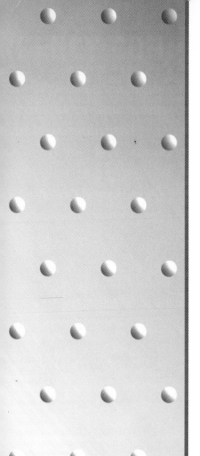

A BUSY NEWSROOM

Thanks to telecommunications, newsroom computers receive up-to-the-minute stories from reporters all over the world. Recordings of world events are bounced around the planet by satellite in seconds.

Television news reports are received in a television switching center.

Reporting In

Newspaper reporters used to send in their stories by dictating them over the telephone. Now, they write news stories on a portable computer, link the computer to a telephone line, and send the text straight to the newspaper's offices.

On the Air

Broadcasters can prepare news items so quickly that a news program's contents can be changed while it is actually being broadcast. Video footage, phoned-in reports, and live interviews can be on the air within minutes.

The contents and order of items in news programs continue to be changed until the last moment so that the news is up to the minute.

LOOKING AHEAD

In the future, we will see more equipment linked together by radio, invisible light beams, and fiber-optic cables instead of wires. The Internet and the World Wide Web will continue to grow as more people, companies, and organizations go on-line.

Buying and selling on the Web, called e-commerce, will become a more important way of doing business.

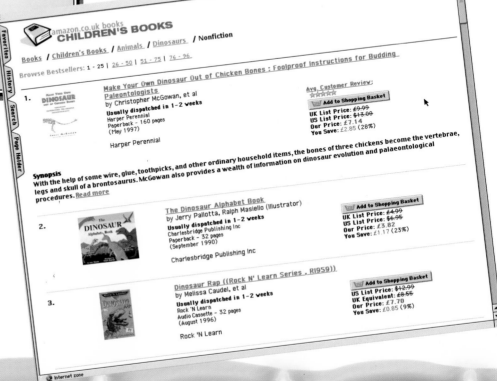

Web TV

Television sets will become more like computers. It is already possible to buy a set-top box that lets you get on-line to the Web using an ordinary TV set without the need for a computer. Soon television sets will be able to do this without an extra box.

Faster computers and quicker Internet connections mean that tomorrow we will communicate faster and more easily than ever, wherever we are.

GLOSSARY

analog Using ever-changing electric currents or radio waves to carry information.

antenna A metal rod or dish used to send or receive radio waves.

attitude The position of an aircraft or spacecraft—the way it tilts, the direction in which it points.

CCTV Closed Circuit Television, a type of video system that sends pictures from video cameras to a video screen or a few video screens.

cordless Linked together without wires, by radio for example.

data Information, especially information used by computers.

digital Using digits (numbers) to carry information.

e-commerce Electronic business, buying and selling done on the Internet.

e-mail Short for "electronic mail," messages sent from one computer to another, especially using the Internet.

equator An imaginary line around the middle of the Earth.

ground station A large dish-shaped aerial on the ground. It is used to send information to a satellite or spacecraft by radio and to receive information in the same way.

Internet A computer network that stretches around the world.

modem A box that helps to link a computer to a telephone line so that it can communicate with other computers.

network A group of computers linked together so that they can share programs or information.

orbit The endless path of a satellite around and around the Earth.

pager A small device that can receive short text messages by radio.

radar A system for finding out where planes and boats are by firing radio waves in all directions and picking up any "reflections" that bounce back.

radio wave A wave of energy that can carry information through space at the speed of light.

rocket A craft that can travel in space, moved by a jet of hot gas produced by burning fuel.

telegraph An early way of sending information as an electric current along a wire or wires.

World Wide Web A huge library of pages of information stored in computers all over the world, linked together so that people can find the pages and look at them easily.

FURTHER READING

Langille, Jacqueline, and Bobbie Kalman. *The Space Shuttle*. Crabtree, 1998.
Oxlade, Chris. *Space*. Children's, 1999.
Parker, Steve. *Satellites*. Raintree Steck-Vaughn, 1997.
Vogt, Gregory. *Space Stations*. Bridgestone, 1999.
Walker, Niki. *Satellites and Space Probes*. Crabtree, 1998.

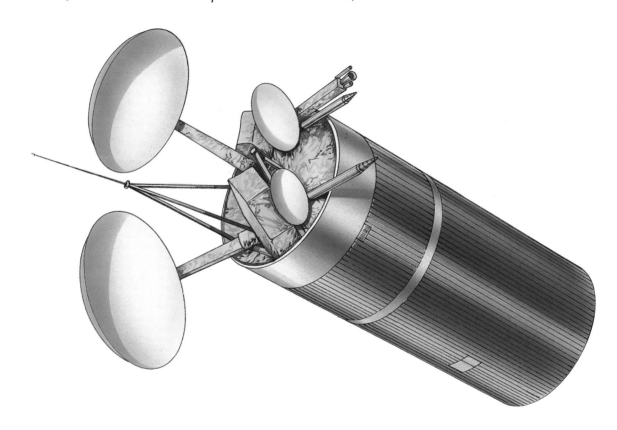

Picture Acknowledgments:
The publishers would like to thank the following for permission to reproduce their pictures:
7 top Gary Braasch/Tony Stone Images, 7 bottom Will & Deni Mcintyre/Science Photo Library, 8 Corbis, 12 Ian Shaw/Tony Stone Images, 17 TEK Image/Science Photo Library, 18 top James King-Holmes/Science Photo Library, 18 bottom Weiss Jerrican/Science Photo Library, 21 Ken W. Johns/Science Photo Library, 22 Alexander Tsiaras/Science Photo Library, 25 top Motorola/Science Photo Library, 25 bottom Charles Gupton/The Stock Market, 26 Firefly Productions/The Stock Market

INDEX